SPOILS OF WAR: ODE TO A REFUSENIK MOTHER

SPOILS OF WAR

ODE TO A REFUSENIK MOTHER

MARGARITA KOROL

URBAN POP ART PROJECTS
CHICAGO

Spoils of War: Ode to a Refusenik Mother is an Urban Pop Art Project supported by COJECO's BluePrint Fellowship, which promotes innovative community projects propelling the Russian-speaking Jewish community. The BluePrint Fellowship is part of the Center Without Walls project of COJECO, sponsored by the UJA-Federation of New York and Genesis Philanthropy Group. "Spoils of War: Ode to a Refusenik Mother" was originally published by Tablet Magazine on June 6, 2012 (bit.ly/spoilspoem), and the panels illustrating the poem exhibited at New York City's National Arts Club through the Russian American Foundation's Russian Heritage Month, sponsored by Mayor Bloomberg and the *New York Post.*

This first edition of *Spoils of War: Ode to a Refusenik Mother* is published by Urban Pop Art Projects, a studio providing design services for nonprofits, TV, publishers, producers, magazines, artists, and musicians. Urban Pop Art Projects also consists of a publishing arm as well as musical and journalistic projects.

Urban Pop Art Projects
1516 North Sedgwick Avenue, The Coach House, Chicago, IL 60610

http://www.urbanpopartist.com

© 2012 Margarita Korol
ISBN 978-0615744605

FOR MY MOTHER, ELLA

AND IN LOVING MEMORY OF

OUR MATRIARCH, LALA STOLKIN
1939-2010

AND MY BROTHER ELI KOROL
1996-2011

Thank you isn't enough
To say to a woman
Who risked her life for you.
But it's a start.

Woods.
To see through
To the other side
Requires one to blur
The rigid obstacles
To foresee
A path
Despite the brush

She went by way of Vienna
A route
That promised better
Something
Anything better than this
This waste
Of potential
Energy within the individual
These roots are festering

She went
Alone
Because the others
Could not
Would not
Break
From the system
From the safety
That they knew.

And she took me
Small helpless burden
Sleeping on a train
Onwards to Italy
Where she waited
For more steps
Toward the outside
Life she did not know
But that was hers
Now that the outsiders
Stepped in

Thought:
It is my first.
A woman in her lingerie
Screaming
At a man
And his leg
To which I cling
Vanishes
As she throws clothes
At him and away
In a box
With her heart

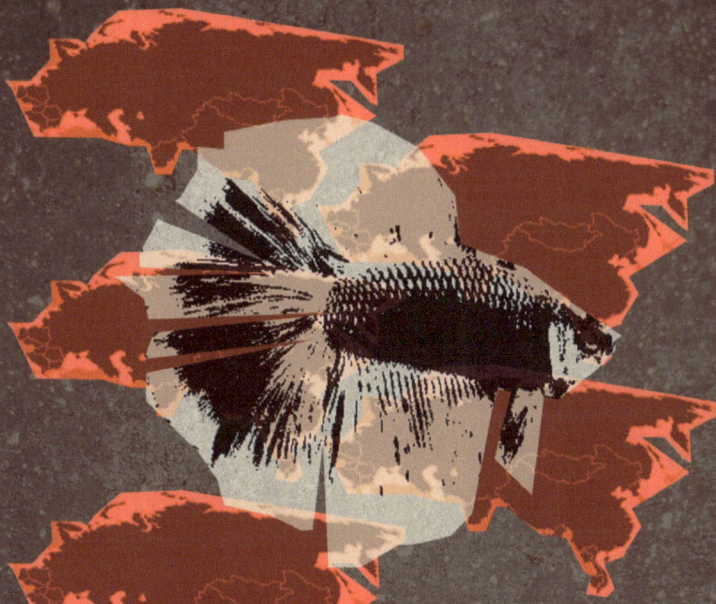

She and me

We leave.

We go away without the people we were to be nuclear with

But it wasn't to be

Not meant to be

Together.

Not fate,

But different spirits.

Beta fish who could not be in a tank with placid others

Where were their fins?

Totalitarian piranhas already bit them off

Or were they without them to begin?

Starfish
Stay and float
But we swam and bit
Against the current
Away.

***

Screaming woman
An image that stayed
In the infant head
And carried through time
Why?
A marital tiff?
Could be traumatic
Divorce is hard on a kid you know.

No
More than that
Bigger
Context:
Political and radioactive

Babushka and Dedushka
Left the year before
Finally
After eight years in wait
Not as persons
In a kafkaesque waiting room
But as pigs
In their shit
Not kosher
It didn't matter
Man didn't care.
No more jobs
I found out
Decades later
Nobody would tell me
Why do you need to know?
America is best country.

Flashback:
Back lash
He said we will wait a year
Convince his people it is the way to go
She waited

His starfish people said no
After a year
So he stayed
Weren't we his people now?
I wondered often
He stayed
Starting over
Making beauty
That I love.

***

KHARKOV

BEFORE:

BEFORE ME THERE WAS THEM
ENGINEERS WHO AS JEWS COULD NOT CATCH A FUCKING BREAK.
BREAKING BACKS FIRST IN SCHOOLS
TO GET THEIR 100%
AND AFTER ORAL EXAMINATIONS
TOLD
THEY WERE NOT GOOD ENOUGH
FROM BIRTH

What to do?
Try again
Fight for
Success
Success of the individual
Bureaucrats run out of official excuses
And must bend and allow
Engineers to become engineers.

When Deda petitioned to leave this place
That hated them
He was refused
And lost steam
Born to a Yiddish actress
Travailing Eastern European borders
With her troop
A pregnant carny
Running away to Kazakstan
Diasporic artists knew
The non-speakers were coming
To take it away
Them and their freedom
But others stayed
Big family turned small
Systematic loyalty killed
Like abused woman staying with man.
Why? No logical answer
Matters of the heart.

Soviet system said to have fucked mother russia's children worse than Hitler

No statistics

Statistics like a good wife loyal to patriarchy

Father Stalin father Yeltsin

Smooth his rage over

Allow it

for his anger

Is worse than this

Whatever this is.

Deda transplanted
And becomes angry man
After escape from East to Midwest
No discussion
A too ugly past
Sad
Lost
Broken and healed over funny
Gnarled knots in the way of pleasantries
Okay, we accept
But not because we knew better
Deprived of context
We did not know

Cultural memory
Starts here
But now I know
Fighter comes out from battle
And to only see ruin
How to think utopically?
Love watered on him still
Maybe anger will be stunted.

Engineering jobs no more

When they said

I am a Jew and I want to go

Back to where I belong

(say what they want to hear

Believe it if you have to)

They said

No—Fuck you

And fuck your degrees

And your families

And your dignity

Traitor

Eight years in wait

In debased lifestyle

Unspeakable

Stories still in pits buried in the woods

Do not dig them up for it is pure

Radioactive pain

Years in wait
His first daughter meets a boy
Love
They marry
No! We are leaving! No new roots!
They say to her
But
Like them she does not listen
Pulls branches toward
individual happiness.

A dream:
What is life if Baba and Deda
Let to go instantly?
Life In Israel?
No, not where they belonged
Opportunists head West
With two young daughters
And two old parents
And others
Schlep to Chicago
Oldest daughter meets American man
No babies yet so better picks
Handsome man
Kind man without soiled fingernails
Nice clean slate
Nice bright future.
Ideal that is illusion.

Choices made
I am born in thick of wait
Thank you father Brezhnev
I owe my existence to your regime.

"long the live MotherLand!"

Same week:
Nuclear meltdown
Sh sh sh national secret
The countrymen must not worry
Must not lose faith in the motherland
May day parade and skeletons dance proving Patriotic loyalty
More waiting yet to leave this dump

She takes plus one
And waits in Italy with it
until Americans say let's go.

Dirty Russians
Take advantage
Of their own
Women in wait
Trickery in the blood
From decades of marination
In croney system
Almost sold as prostitute while
Seeking shelter.
Jewkrainians are a hot item
To Italian slobs
Her instinct said leave
Smells fishy
Another narrow escape.

Another day
To feed buckwheat made on hot plate
To little girl
Free little one does not know
Close your eyes! Sleep!
I remember how
She told me
On the train

Okay. Obedient little girl always
Because I trusted her love
Forgotten potty chair on plane to Chicago
Heartbreak!
This small tragedy a luxury
To girl in new life.
She does not know.
Family says "good."
This is how life should be.
Spoil the milk
for it is rich.

OUR ROCK, OUR HEART

Mama with baby girl
Starts over
Medical training in old country doesn't count here.
Study
Work
Look for love
Found
In men
And lost
Again in heartbreak fruit is picked off trees
Children like sweet cherries
Delicious lives cultivated
She tries
Strong woman
Like her mother
Who was our rock, our heart
Our Matriarch

Still love big in hearts
We grow full of the good life

ASK AND THOU SHALT RECEIVE

I ask

I want to know

What happened

Where are roots from this fruit tree really?

Why do you need to know?

Reading black literature
Jealousy felt for woman
Who has a grasp of her roots

Ugly ugly rings on tree yes.
But with context of trunk
branches strengthen
Fruit flowers
Wisdom and love
Love for new fruit
And love for old root

Found answers
From Brave old men and
women who dig in dirt and
weed pain out
Feeling feeling feeling
In the dirt
It's okay
And thank you to them
By the way

Mother's other babies
Brother and sister
American born
Different perspective
Some Holes though at base
Fruit floating in space

And the paternal sweetness
Transplanted pomegranates in Israel
Now another kind of imported produce to America
Siblings still mine
Ripening and evolving
Tragic kingdom with a fresh fruit fallen innocently without systematic intervention
Even when watered
Even now in the democratic California sun
We are trapped on the tree wishing to have fallen instead
And now must cultivate something in this seeming wasteland of milk and honey

They did not tell you who you are
Roots buried with erasing dirt
Swept under table.
You read and debate
Criticism of big new country
"Down with these imperialists"
Yes!
Good
Opinions grow but
Roots unfound still

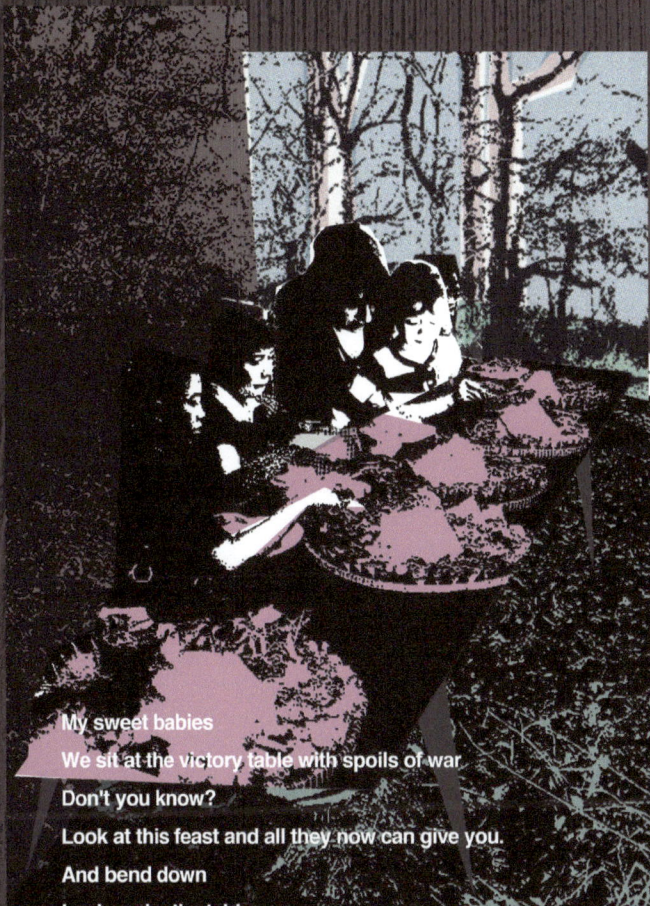

My sweet babies

We sit at the victory table with spoils of war

Don't you know?

Look at this feast and all they now can give you.

And bend down

Look under the table

What is there?

So dirty, but put clean hands in

And feel life turned chalk dead

Clean hands hold power

Bring these fighters at the table honey

Sweet potential energy

From hives of progress
In American schools
And on American streets
And in American offices
Bring it back to them
And know who is eating it.

They are your warriors
They fought and got
All of this
For you

Now eat.

ACKNOWLEDGEMENTS

I would like to personally thank everyone who has contributed to the evolution of the *Spoils of War* project.

To my editors and friends at Tablet Magazine and Nextbook Press, who have extended the reach of this poem, my art, and my Jewkrainian voice. Your work ethic is nothing short of Soviet standards.

To my friends and colleagues at COJECO for allowing my artwork to represent the Russian-speaking Jewish community of New York via the BluePrint Fellowship and beyond.

To Marina and the Russian American Foundation family for sponsoring the *Spoils of War* exhibit at the National Arts Club at Gramercy Park.

To Susan Green for her activist work in the 80s on behalf of Soviet Jewish refuseniks. She was our megaphone and continues to be an inspiration to action.

To Yuri Tarnopolsky, my grandparents' dear friend and fellow dissident who refused to be silenced then, and was gracious in answering my questions. He provided the world with the gift of refusenik cultural memory in his book, *Memoirs of 1984*, and taught me that we are not victims but victors. He thanked my grandparents in his book, and I am compelled to thank him too.

To Gal Beckerman and other contemporary American and immigrant writers sharing general and personal histories of the plight of Soviet Jewry. Thanks to them for their research and wisdom.

To my Stolkin family for their strength and courage in the face of dark circumstances as refuseniks. They are all my heroes. On behalf of my siblings, I thank my mother's, grandparents' and great-grandparents' generations for their personal sacrifices.

To my Korol family for being a joyful presence in my life. Even in the face of totalitarian and universal strains, I will always be loyal to the creativity and humanitarian love that you have taught me to foster.

And finally, to my dear friends and colleagues in Chicago, New York, Los Angeles, and beyond for rallying around Urban Pop Art Projects. I strive to color your world at our studio.

ABOUT MARGARITA KOROL

Margarita Korol is an artist, writer and the founder of Urban Pop Art Projects, a studio creating art for other artists, musicians, and community organizations in order to amplify the humanitarian work they are doing in New York City, Chicago, and Los Angeles.

Born the week of Chernobyl in Ukraine to refuseniks, Korol's focus on empowering individuals in disadvantaged struggles against their political systems is an ongoing theme in her work. Before her 2012 *Spoils of War* exhibit at New York's National Arts Club, her exhibit at the New York Aquarium in Fall 2011 for ArtOnBrighton featured a series of propaganda posters directed to her generation of Russian-speaking Jewish immigrants. Previously, *Propaglasnost: The Transparency Projects* series promoting active democracy and political transparency for the 25th anniversary of Chernobyl was on view at NYC's KGB Bar spring and summer of 2011. Meanwhile, her installation commemorating the 20th anniversary of the fall of the Berlin Wall, *Die Mauer,* is housed at Chicago's DANK-Haus German Cultural Center.